DICTION III: THE PARADOX OF REFLECTION

DICTION III: THE PARADOX OF REFLECTION

A Dictionary of Thought

by J. A. Gucci

First Edition, 2026

ISBN: 979-8-9946751-8-2

Printed in the United States of America

Book III of The Paradox Trilogy:
Feeling — Faith — Thought

TABLE OF CONTENTS

SECTION I — DIALECTIC
Every question is a mirror; every answer a crack.

SECTION II — TRANSCENDENCE
When the mirror breaks, reflection remains.

"Every silence is load bearing."

SECTION I — DIALECTIC

Every question is a mirror; every answer a crack.

WONDER

WOMAN
What does that cloud look like?

MAN
That's a sad clown.
(*pause*)
What about that one?

WOMAN
That's a riddle:
"I am light at the edge—
darkness within."

MAN
Maybe the clown and the riddle
are truth—
wearing mirrors.

WOMAN
Hm.

MAN
And that one?

WOMAN
That…
is a riddle.

Command: Let the question outlive the answer.

MYSTERY

WOMAN
The moon is envious tonight.

MAN
I see.

WOMAN
What do you see?

MAN
A smirky smile.

WOMAN
Where?

MAN
There.

WOMAN
No—
there.

MAN
There?

WOMAN
Right…
there.

(A vein of light cuts the cloud.)

MAN
Admiration.

WOMAN
Rivalry.

MAN
Mimicry.

Command: Name the unknown, and it changes shape.

KNOWLEDGE

MAN
Can I get to 5th Avenue
on the N line?

CLERK
No.

MAN
B line?

CLERK
That's not gonna do it either.

MAN
I must be in the wrong station.

CLERK
That's three wrongs in a row, pal.

MAN
It's Christmas.
Help me, will ya?

PIGEON
Take it east…
Take it west…

MAN
Say something meaningful—
please!

CLERK
An arrow in flight
is always at rest.

PIGEON
Let it snow…

*Command: Ask for directions; learn that nowhere is a
stop along the way.*

LOGIC

BOY
I did it.

ADULT
You're admitting
to stealing the chocolate.

BOY
No.
That was a lie.

ADULT
So—
you're lying now.

BOY
No sir…
I'm telling the truth.

CHOCOLATE (*quietly*)
Peanuts.

Command: Reason circles the drain; taste what's left.

PERCEPTION

WOMAN
Where are you?

MAN
Here.

WOMAN
Which way?

MAN
This way.

WOMAN
I'm coming.

MAN
Did you find me yet?

WOMAN
No.

MAN
Don't move.
I'll come to you.

WOMAN
Still tethered.

MAN
By what?

WOMAN
By voice.

MAN
By thread.

Command: Every distance begins with a sound.

TRUTH

JUDGE
Jurors—
we have come
to the crucial point:
deliberations.

Your decision—
to fry,
or not to fry—
this guy—
the defendant,
by way of electrocution,
injection,
guillotine—
whatever the warden's serving today.

For the crimes
he has been charged with—
murder,
maybe first,
second—
doesn't matter.

Remember:
facts only.
Lies aren't facts—
unless a fact is a lie.
Capisce?

Everyone gets a fair trial.
Not perfect—

but fair.
Because that's how we do it.
Fact.

Now, I'm going to lunch.
The facts there are sliced, roasted,
layered on Italian bread,
with fries.
Waffle cut.
Or maybe tuna salad.

Good luck, jurors.

Command: Eat what's served; truth was always on the menu.

INTUITION

LES
listen man—

MONK
I know.

LES
You don't know shit.

MONK
I know a lotta shit, man.

LES
Not this shit.

MONK
Man, I've been a bandleader
my whole life.
You ain't the first
to tell me this shit.

LES
You ain't shittin' me?

MONK
Shit—
I know dullsville when I see it.
It's a snoozefest.

LES
I love you, man—
this shit ain't about you.

MONK
Don't give me that shit.
It ain't never personal.

LES
You're full of shit.

MONK
Brother man—
take your shit,
play that shit.
They're lucky to have you
and your shit.
And that ain't no shit.

LES
Shit.

MONK
We're gonna miss your shit around here.

LES
Now that's some shit right there.

MONK
Shit—
we better get back to that shit
before I catch a lotta shit from the guys.

LES
I'll miss… this shit.

MONK
Me too, man.
This shit.

LES
C'mon.
Let's go play that shit.

Command: Trust the noise that never asks for proof.

REASON

SPOKESPERSON
Pragmathematically speaking—
I've got
unfortunate news.

It seems…
the prize—
the new luxury car we promised—
…has been stolen.

That's right, folks.
Gone.

Don't let your engines overheat.
Resol is gobsmacked
to make this right.

If anyone here today
requested an interview
yesterday,
or the day before today,
or—today—
because you knew
this was going to happen…

Well—
nobody could metaphysically fathom
that anything like this would happen, right?

Therefore,
knowing that you didn't,
is proof.
Proof!

If no interview was requested—
a refund
shan't be given.

Resol will be enchanted
to provide one,
of course.
Just form a line here.
We'll take good care of you.
Promise.

No requests, heh?
I am…
flaggerblasted.

Well—
those are the brakes, folks.
Though some say
the brakes were never installed.
Others say
the ride is still going.

And me?
I'm just here
to announce the winners.

Which, metaphorically speaking,
includes everyone here.
Especially—
the losers.

Command: Applaud the logic that drives in circles; it still gets you home.

WISDOM

FRED
Zero. Zip. Zilch.

TIM
You're a lousy accountant, Fred.

FRED
It's not me, Tim—
your earnings are too high.

TIM
I was counting on that refund
to pay the mortgage.

FRED
I have no room—
don't even ask.

TIM
Smear a number or two, will you?

FRED
Sorry—
I'm a straight shooter, Tim.

TIM
I'll lose my house, Fred.

FRED
Then do your own taxes.
I only file returns
for people
who do not file their own.

Command: The wise fix no accounts they cannot also unmake.

DOUBT

HELIX
Excuse me, sir—
which way to the Infinity Theater?

MAN 1
Any which-way path
will do, sir.

HELIX
That's impossible.

MAN 1
Precisely.

———

HELIX
Excuse me, sir—
how do I get to the Infinity Theater?

MAN 2
Ha!
Is this a joke?

HELIX
Not a jo—

MAN 2
You must've knotted
your brain in loops.

———

HELIX
Ma'am?
The Infinity Theater?

WOMAN
That's life, I suppose.
Loops.
Goodness.
Espresso.
The good ol' days…

HELIX
Yes, but—

WOMAN
Half the way.
Then a quarter.
Then an eighth.
Then a sixteenth.
Then—

HELIX
Excuse me…?

WOMAN
Then a thirty-second…
a sixty-fourth…
one-two-hundred-fifty-sixth…

HELIX
Which way—?

WOMAN
That is—the way.

Command: Every answer widens the question.

PARADOX

JOEY
I gathered us here today
to talk about Harry's birthday.
Only problem is—
Harry doesn't exist.

Not dead.
Just never was.

But he's a dear friend.
You understand.

HARRY
Hi everyone.
Everything Joey said—true.
All of it.

I was never born.
No record. No witness.
The fire took the hospital.
The people who knew me are gone.
There's no proof.

And yet—
here I am.
Not existing.
In front of you.

JOEY
You may be asking:
"What's the party for?"

Simple.

A celebration
of someone who isn't here
by people
who might not be either.

Now tell me this—
if he never existed…

Why is there blood
on that cushion?

*Command: When nothing adds up, count again—
something is hiding in the sum.*

MEANING

[Rehearsal room — bass hums, cymbals flicker, sheet music folded.]

AL
Hey uh…
Chief?

BEN
Yeah, Al?

AL
How d'ya…
want me to play…
the axe-idental in bar ninety-one…
beat three and a half?

BEN
Why would you ask me that?

AL
It's a B-flat.
Then the same note—
comes back up an octave.
No accidental.

CAL
Oh here we go…

BEU
Divine logos in gullies.

CAL
Pick one, man.

BEU
Just play the fuckin' note Ben.

CAL
Which ever you choose—

BEU
That's the one you play—

CAL
That's the right answer—

BEN
Hold it!
(silence)
What the fuck are you trying to say, Al?

(silence)

AL
I gotta take a piss.

Command: When meaning breaks down, the body writes
the final note.

(The score ends where the hand begins.)

MIND

[Dental chair hums. Fluorescent light flickers. A slow drip from the rinse basin.]

DENTIST
Mirror.

MR. MOLAR
Here you go.

DENTIST
Explorer.

MR. MOLAR
Right here.

DENTIST
Probe.

MR. MOLAR
You got it.

Command: Thought hands the tools that carve it.

SECTION II — TRANSCENDENCE
When the mirror breaks, reflection remains.

CONSCIOUSNESS

MIRROR
Who are you?

MAN
The name is—

MIRROR
No.
Let's try again.
(pause)
Who
are you?

MAN
Matter.

MIRROR
No, no.
Go deeper.

MAN
Essence.

MIRROR
Closer.
You are not ego.
You are not name.
You are not form.
You are not thought.

MAN
I am you.
MIRROR
Then who
am I?

MAN
The question.

*Command: Look long enough, and the eye becomes the
asking.*

MEMORY

CLERK
No.

MANAGER
Check again.

CLERK
No, no.

MANAGER
Try Lloyd.

CLERK
No, no, no.

MANAGER
Schmidt?

CLERK
No.

MANAGER
Pozo.

CLERK
…Yes.

MANAGER
Knew it.

CLERK
But—no Pozo either.
MANAGER
Wait—what?

CLERK
Yes.

MANAGER
Yes?

CLERK
No.

MANAGER
Stop.

CLERK
No!

MANAGER
Yes!

CLERK
Knock it off!

MANAGER
No!
Yes!

Command: What returns is never what you lost—only what endures the search.

SELF

HOST
Welcome, everyone.
Please—
enjoy the party.
Just be yourselves.

MAN 1
Hello.

WOMAN
Hi there.

MAN 2
Good evening.

WOMAN
Lovely gathering.

MAN 2
Very nice.

MAN 1
Yes, indeed.

(Pause)

WOMAN
Whoopsies!

MAN 1
I'm a neurosurgeon—
you look pale.

MAN 2
Did you fall?
I'm a lawyer.

WOMAN
Let's tidy that shirt—
napkin under the chin.

MAN 1
Say "ahh."

MAN 2
If it was an accident,
you had a case.

WOMAN
All squeaky clean now!

HOST
Just be yourselves!

GUN
Who wants to play—
roulette?

(*The air changes. Jazz slows. Lights dim. Guests still.*)

MAN 2
Mauled by a Maltese.

WOMAN
No good.

MAN 1
I never wanted
to be a doctor.

MAN 2
Flesh from limb.

WOMAN
At mothering.

MAN 1
I did it
for my mother.

MAN 2
Debonair to distortion.
Woman
At cooking.

MAN 1
I loathe her.
I'll take her life.
I'll take mine.

MAN 2
Masks over masks—
I.

WOMAN
Pretty please?

HOST
Just be yourselves!

GUN
Any takers?

(Rewind sound. Jazz resumes. Lights up. Reset.)

MAN 1
Hello.

WOMAN
Hi there.

MAN 2
Good evening.

WOMAN
Lovely gathering.

MAN 2
Very nice.

MAN 1
Yes, indeed.

HOST
Just be yourselves!

GUN
Never mind.
Time already pulled the trigger.

*Command: When the masks fall off, rewind; the self
prefers a practiced truth.*

BEING

WOMAN
The scent—before the bite.

MAN
Repetition. Pretending permanence.

WOMAN
You are mistaken.

(The pigeon does not fly.)

MAN
I was the center.

WOMAN
I was the edge.

MAN
When one leans—into the other.

WOMAN
I was the water.

MAN
Grounded.
Woman
Up and away.

MAN
Déjà vu.

WOMAN
Tethered—by thread.

(A balloon is released. Another is kept.)

MAN
Ashes clinging to the hearth.

WOMAN
Do you ever wonder if the shadow of your chair is
more aware of time than you are?

MAN
Silence has weight—it crushes us, and keeps us
afloat.

Command: Existence leans; let the weight be shared.

NOTHINGNESS

(The graves are side by side. The stones are swapped.)

(The circling begins.)

WOMAN
Burden.

MAN
Carry the absence of meaning.

WOMAN
Permanence.

MAN
As if it were—a grave.

WOMAN
Impossibility.

*(The circling never ends. The burden does not lighten.
Time passes by footstep and breath.)*

MAN
Which one—is me?

WOMAN
Which one—is I?

*(The mirrors mimic each other, then abandon their
source.
The self watches itself dissolve.)*

All
We are not here.
We are the here.

Command: Let the void name you; the rest is echo.

BECOMING

MAN
I reach—

WOMAN
I answer—

(The figures blur. Identity softens.)

MAN
If I dissolve—
do you remain?

WOMAN
If you dissolve—
who am I?

(The line between image and real collapses.
The moment becomes more real than the person.)

All
We are not here.
We are the here.
(A faint shimmer. A breath. A blackout.)

Command: Dissolve the border; emerge in the blur.

Colophon

This volume was set in a serif typeface chosen for clarity under constraint and printed on acid-free paper.

Diction III completes the Diction trilogy.

Printed in the United States.

www.ingramcontent.com/pod-product-compliance
Lightning Source LLC
Chambersburg PA
CBHW051502140726
47987CB00006B/2836